The Lost Rabbit

Story by

Peter Brownlow

Illustrated by

A. Fairclough

All the young rabbits were outside of their burrow
jumping, running and chasing each
other all around the meadow.

They ran down hill

then ran up hill.

Ran in and out of thick bushes and even played hide and seek.

One of the younger rabbits thought she had found the best place to hide, inside a bramble bush, and sat quietly waiting to be found. She waited and waited and waited.

The sun went down and all around the young rabbit was darkness, so she settled down to sleep wondering why no-one had found her.

The next morning the young rabbit came out of the bramble bush to find her friends but there was nobody about and she did not know the way home.

She spotted a small blue bird stood on a tree branch.

"Excuse me," said the young rabbit, "can you help me? I'm lost."

The blue bird looked the young rabbit up and down and replied, "Sure. Where do you want to go?"

"I want to go home," said the young rabbit. The blue bird turned his head sideways and said, "And where is home?"

"I want to go to the meadow with the big oak tree on top of a hill," said the young rabbit.

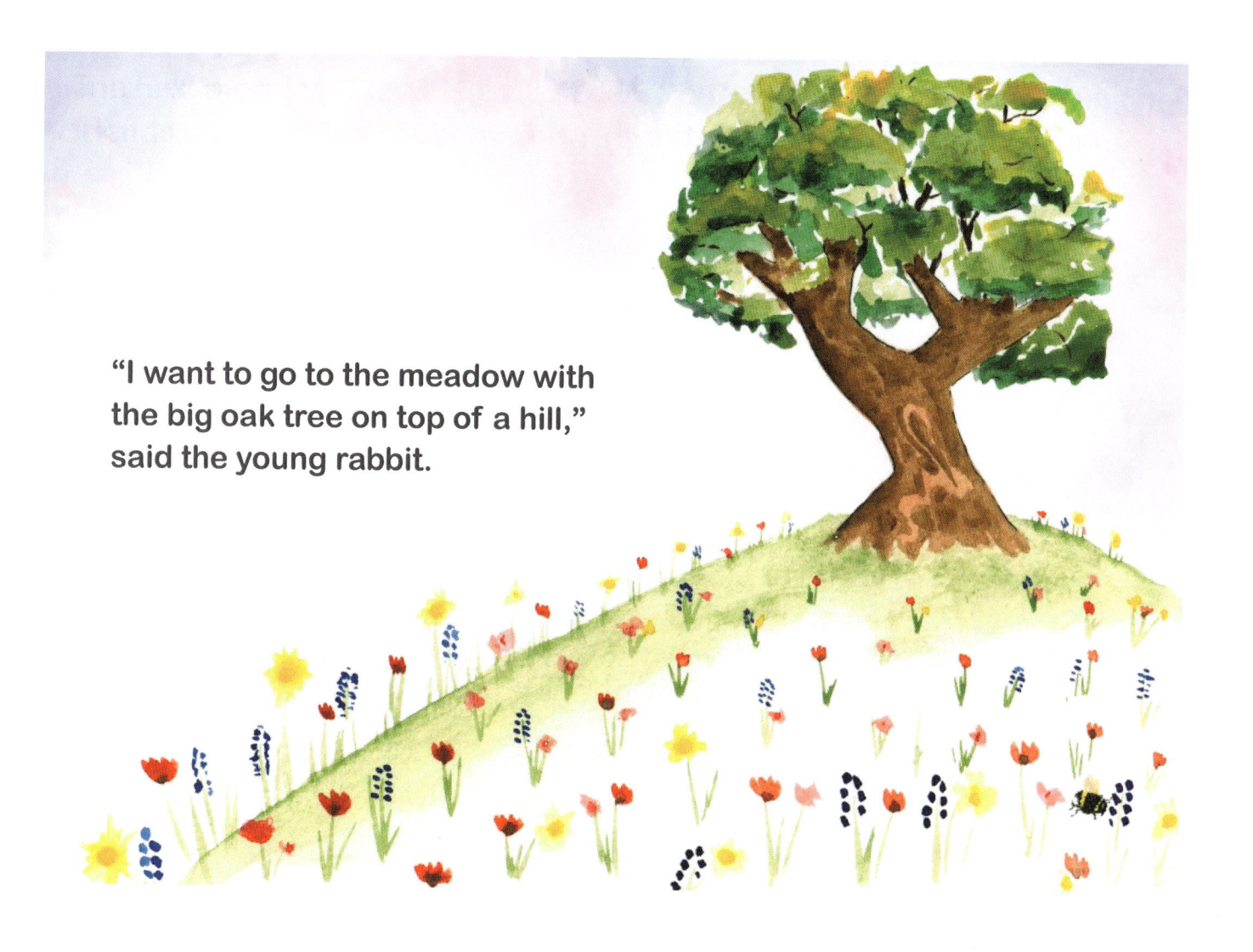

"I know where that is. Follow me."

The blue bird flew high up into the sky and the young rabbit followed but soon lost sight of the blue bird, she could not follow him because she cannot fly.

So the young rabbit was lost even more and thought she would never see home again.

A mole suddenly appeared out of the ground.
"Excuse me," said the young rabbit, "can you help me? I'm lost."

The mole squinted his eyes, looked the young rabbit up and down and replied, "Sure. Where do you want to go?"

"I want to go ho.."
the young rabbit stopped herself
and shook her head,
"No, I want to go to the meadow
with the big oak tree on top of a hill."

"I know where that is. Follow me."
The mole dived back underground and started to dig a tunnel.

The young rabbit followed but although the young rabbit could also dig tunnels she was unable to keep up with the mole as he was digging too fast.

So the young rabbit was lost even more and thought she would never see the meadow again.

She climbed out of the mole hole and saw a squirrel on the ground eating a nut. "Excuse me," said the young rabbit, "can you help me? I'm lost."

The squirrel put down his nut, looked the young rabbit up and down and replied, "Sure. Where do you want to go?"

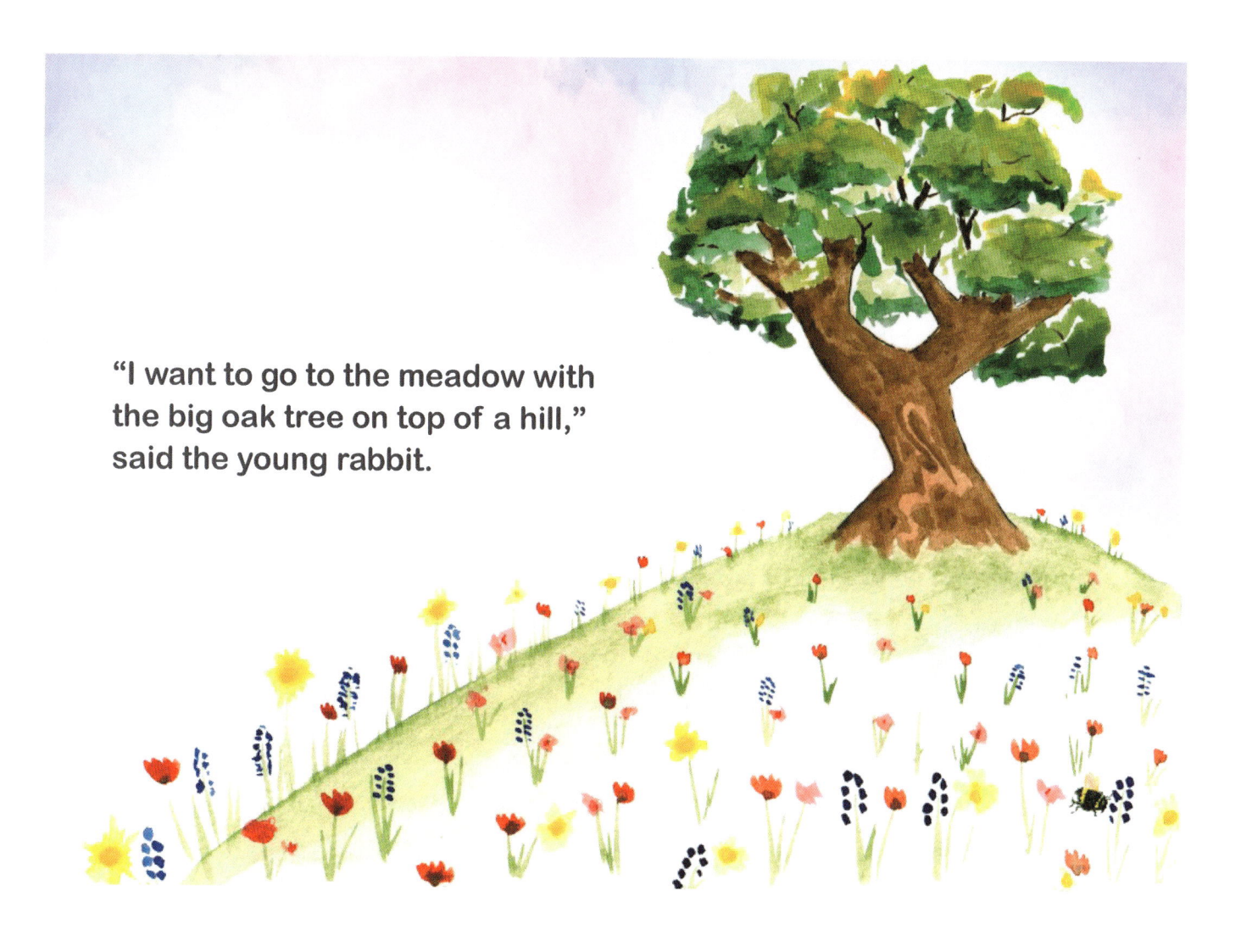

"I want to go to the meadow with the big oak tree on top of a hill," said the young rabbit.

"I know where that is. Follow me."

The squirrel jumped up into a tree and started to run, leaping from branch to branch, tree to tree.

The young rabbit could not follow the squirrel because she cannot climb trees and leap from branches.

So the young rabbit was lost even more and thought she would never see her mother again.

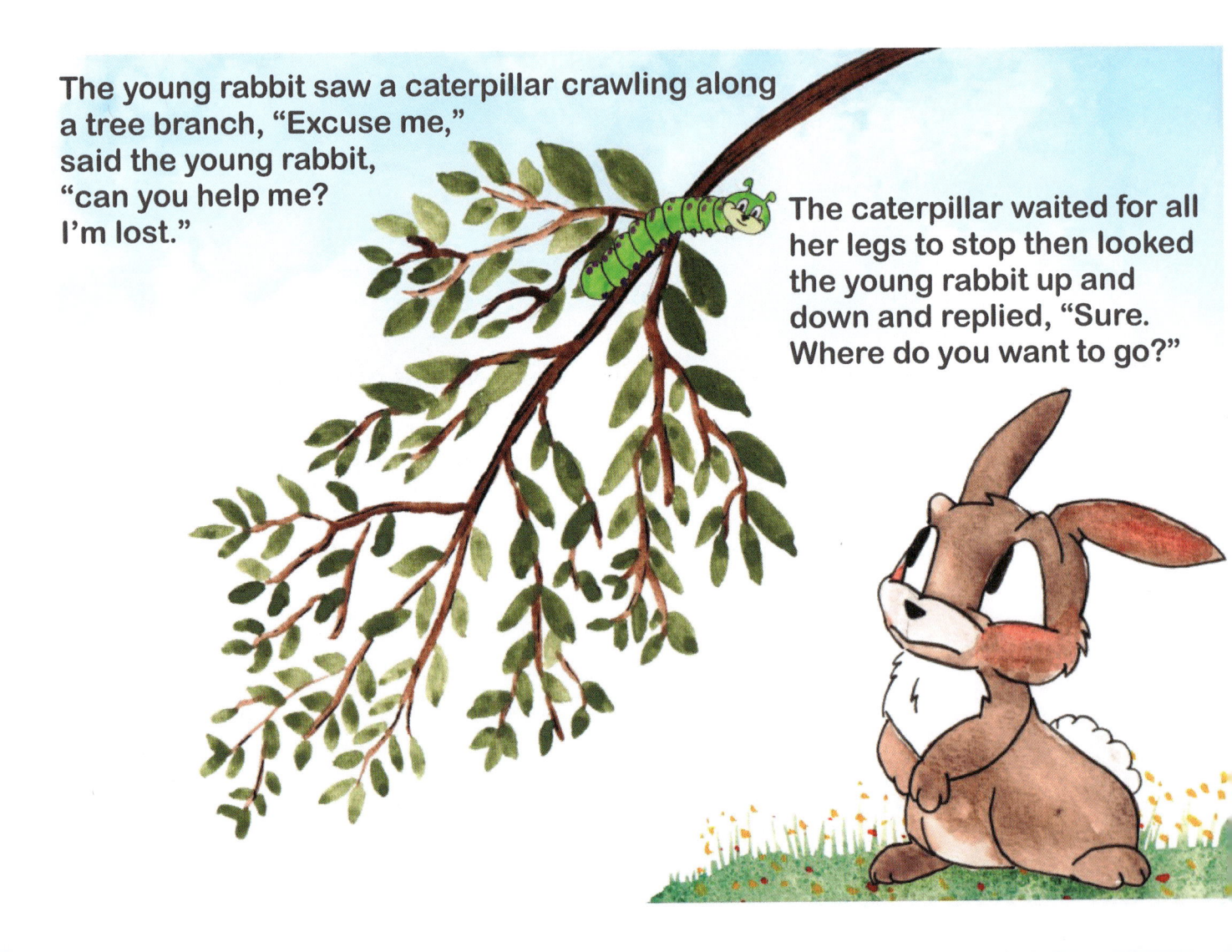

The young rabbit saw a caterpillar crawling along a tree branch, "Excuse me," said the young rabbit, "can you help me? I'm lost."

The caterpillar waited for all her legs to stop then looked the young rabbit up and down and replied, "Sure. Where do you want to go?"

"I want to go to the meadow with the big oak tree on top of a hill," said the young rabbit.

"I know where that is. Just wait a few minutes and I will take you."

The young rabbit waited and watched the caterpillar close her eyes and turn into a cocoon.

The young rabbit waited and watched the caterpillar, who was now a cocoon.

And saw her change and emerge as a beautiful butterfly.

"Follow me," said the butterfly and flew high into the air.

Suddenly a gust of wind caught the butterfly and blew her far away and the young rabbit lost sight of her.

So the young rabbit was lost even more and thought she would never see her father again.

The young rabbit came across a stream and saw a water vole. "Excuse me," said the young rabbit, "can you help me? I'm lost."

The water vole wiped his eyes, looked the young rabbit up and down and replied, "Sure. Where do you want to go?"

"I want to go to the meadow with the big oak tree on top of a hill," said the young rabbit.

"I know where that is. Follow me." The water vole jumped into the stream and swam across to the other side.

The rabbit was about to follow but a strong current caught the water vole and sent him tumbling over a waterfall.

The water vole cried, "Yippee!" with delight, sounding like he was having a lot of fun and disappeared out of sight.

But the young rabbit was not having fun because she was still lost...

...and was feeling hungry.

The young rabbit saw a snail by the bank of the stream.
"Excuse me," said the young rabbit, "can you help me? I'm lost."

The snail slowly turned her head, looked the young rabbit up and down and replied, "Sure. Where do you want to go?"

"I want to go to the meadow with the big oak tree on top of a hill," said the young rabbit.

"I know where that is. Follow me." The snail slowly turned round and slowly started to move forward. And the young rabbit followed.

But snail was so slow that the young rabbit got frustrated and shouted at the snail to...

Hurry up!!

The startled snail disappeared into her shell
and refused to come out.

So the young rabbit was still lost and started to feel cold
then she started to cry.

A fox suddenly appeared, looked the young rabbit up and down and asked, "Are you lost? Would you like some help?"

Sobbing the young rabbit replied, "Yes, I am lost. I want to get back to the meadow with the big oak tree on top of a hill."

"Oh, I know where that is," said the fox slyly.

"Follow me."

The fox headed off towards a large dark forest.

Thisssss way

"This way," he said.

As they entered the forest a group of crows saw the fox and swooped down worried that he was after their eggs.

The crows chased him out of the forest and across a field but the young rabbit could not keep up.

And watched the fox and the crows disappear over a hill with a big oak tree.

So now she was totally lost and looking around she did not know where she was, she sighed heavily and started to cry again.

Suddenly two fluffy ears appeared over a small mound in front of her.

Then another two...

...then some more. They were rabbits, she had found her way home. She must have wandered around in a big circle.

Oh, she was so very happy.

The other rabbits asked her where she had been and that they were all worried about her.

The young rabbit said that she had been on an adventure and asked if the other rabbits wanted to hear about it.

"Oh, yes. Oh, yes please tell us," they all cried. So they all settled down on the meadow under the big oak tree on top of a hill to hear all about the young rabbit's tale.

Peter lives on the edge of the West Pennine moors with his wife Debbie and dog Rosie. He has written other children's books including The First Frog and The First Lamb.

Alicia, from Lancashire, is mum to two children and one fluffball they call Luna. Alicia is studying for her second degree, a BA in Illustration.

Printed in Great Britain
by Amazon